"Howdee—ee!"

CHRISTMAS AT GRINDERS SWITCH

CHRISTMAS
AT GRINDERS SWITCH

Ophelia Colley Cannon

Minnie Pearl, pseud.

WITH AN INTRODUCTION BY ROY ACUFF
ILLUSTRATED BY JIM PADGETT

ABINGDON PRESS • NASHVILLE

CHRISTMAS AT GRINDERS SWITCH

Library of Congress Cataloging in Publication Data

Minnie Pearl.
  Christmas at Grinders Switch.
  1. Christmas—Anecdotes, facetiae, satire, etc.
I. Title.
PN623.C36M56 1985   818'.5402   85-11073

ISBN 0-687-07775-3
ISBN 0-687-07776-1 (pbk.: alk. paper)

This book was printed on acid-free paper.

MANUFACTURED BY
THE PARTHENON PRESS, AT NASHVILLE,
TENNESSEE, UNITED STATES OF AMERICA

To
my family—*all of them*—
with memories of many
happy Christmases

INTRODUCTION

This is a real privilege to reminisce and write a few words about one of my best friends in the entertainment world, also one of my family's best friends in private life.

Most people would expect if they met or had a phone call from Minnie Pearl they would hear a loud "How-dee!" That is not true. The only time you will hear that expression from her is on the stage to an audience. On the phone you would hear a very soft and gentle voice saying "hello," and that would be the voice of Mrs. Henry Cannon, who has portrayed the character of Minnie Pearl, a lovable little country girl from Grinders Switch, Tennessee, for forty-four years.

Ever since I first introduced her on the Grand Ole Opry, in 1940, she has been known to millions of people who love her as Minnie Pearl and one of the best-known personalities in show business.

At that time she was known to her many friends as Ophelia Colley, a lovable young lady who had just graduated from Ward-Belmont College, at that time a girls' school.

A short time later, she met and married a fine young man, Henry Cannon, who was a World War II veteran and successful businessman and skilled pilot. I have flown many miles with both of them in their private plane to personal appearances all over the country. We were among the first country groups to fly the Atlantic Ocean to entertain our boys in the service—flown by the U.S. Air Force to Wiesbaden, Germany, and other European posts in 1949.

As I watch Minnie work today on the Opry stage or on some of the network shows, I see her as the same person who came to the Opry in 1940. She has had a very interesting life both as Minnie Pearl and as Mrs. Henry Cannon.

I am sure you will enjoy her reminiscences in this book.

Roy Acuff

Roy Acuff

Christmas is the happiest time of all the year at Grinders Switch. We're happy there, most generally, anyway, but at Christmastime there's a extra special glow that sorta spreads all the way from Ceph Jones's General Store to Lem Perkins's pasture at the edge of town and back again.

Uncle Nabob always says if we could jest hold onto a little of that Christmasy feeling all year 'round we wouldn't hafta worry about no atomic bomb or none of that fightin' bizness. He's a great believer in peaceful dealin's with folks. He's a little feller, and he ain't never been one to take on much over fightin'. Unk says if we could jest learn to git along with the fellers that live next door and the ones acrost the hollow, maybe we could git along with the folks in foreign lands. I don't know but what he's right. As far as I'm concerned, I love my fellowmen—I love the fellers and I love the men!

Love's a pretty interesting thing to talk about at Christmas or any time. 'Specially at Christmas. Ever since I was a youngun Mammy allus told us about how important it was to celebrate Christmas as the birthday of the little Lord Jesus instead of a "gift gittin' " time. She allus tried to explain to us

about how God loved us so much that he gave the onliest Son he had so that we might have the Everlasting Life. Her and my pappy loved one another and wanted me and Sister and Brother to love one another too. Now that ain't easy, what with Sister always a-borrowin' your hair ribbons and Brother puttin' frogs in your bed. But leastways we tried, with the help of a little peachtree switch or two.

But at Christmastime it seemed easier. We'd begin gittin' that Christmas feeling way back in the fall when we started looking at the catalogues and trying to earn a little money to buy gifts. Me and Sister uster run errands and crack walnuts and do all sorts of chores fer the neighbors. We sorta enjoyed it—but not Brother. Like Unk allus said, some folks has got git up and go—the only git up and go Brother has is git up and go eat breakfast and git up and go back to bed. Even when he was a little feller and Mammy'd tell him to lay in the wood—that's where we'd find him—layin'—sound asleep—in the woodpile. So at Christmastime he never had much money ahead—then or now. Like Unk says, Brother ain't a failure, he jest started at the bottom and he likes it there.

One Christmas I did think he'd kinda got a little stirred up over earnin' a little money fer a present to give a girl. They was a girl name of Elvirey O'Beury come a-visitin' Lucy Satterfield. Elvirey was from Shady Grove about twenty-five mile away from Grinders Switch. She was a sorta citified girl with permanented hair (sorta store-boughten reddish color, it seemed to me, but I never named it to nobody!) and a stylish look to her.

Brother has allus went along to the parties with me and my feller, Hezzie. That wasn't to my likin', but Mammy allus made me look out fer Brother. It wasn't so bad when I was a little girl, but since me and Hezzie have been keepin' company it's been a real drawback to courtin' to have Brother allus in listenin' distance when we go some place. Sweet nothin's is hard to come by when there's a audience. Hezzie's shy anyway. I have a hard enough time gittin' a compliment outa him when we're by ourselves.

Lucy had a Christmas party and all us young folks got a invite. Anyway, that particular night when we walked in Lucy's front room and Brother seen Elvirey, I stopped dead in my tracks. I allus knowed love would find a way, but I never knowed it would find Brother. Well, it did. Brother got a look on his face like a mule with the blind staggers. He jest set his eyes on Elvirey and never unset 'em.

And then somebody suggested that we play "Post Office." It might of been me; it's my favorite game. Brother worked it around to where he was to kiss

Elvirey. Well, he kissed her all right—and fell backwards in a dead faint! The fellers toted him out and stuck his head in the horse trough. It was a short love affair. Later Brother told a bunch of the fellers down around the General Store that he didn't care fer that love stuff; said it was too dangerous.

Anyway, as a result he didn't hafta git her a Christmas present after all. Maybe it was jest as well. Elvirey turned out to be a real flirt. Hoke Weatherby was real took with her, and he writ her a letter every day fer a month or so after she left. I seen Hoke the other day and ast him how the courtship was a-makin' out. He said not too good. Seems like since Hoke'd been a-writin' all them letters to her, Elvirey'd fell in love with the *mailman* and was a-marryin' him next June! So maybe it worked out jest as well fer Brother to not get too stuck on her after all.

Gittin' the gifts all ready and the decorations up was so excitin' we could hardly sleep at night. Me and Sister allus tried to think of somethin' real nice to give folks. Brother was kinda hard to get Christmas gifts fer. I said to Uncle Nabob jest last Christmas, I said, "I wish I could git Brother somethin' he's never had before," and Unk says, "Why don't you git him a steady job?"

I remember the first time we got him a store-boughten suit. It had two pairs of pants! That was nice fer the winter, but wearin' both pairs got awful hot come summer. He don't do much fer clothes, and they don't seem to help him a lot. Mammy don't encourage none of us to put too much store in clothes. She says clothes don't make the man, and Uncle Nabob says nope, but you shore can go a lot of places with 'em that you can't go without 'em!

I remember when we got Brother's Christmas-present suit, because the first time he wore it was the first time me and Brother ever rode a train. We went down to the depot but we couldn't figure out which end of the train to get on—both of 'em had

stopped. We've got a train that comes through
Grinders Switch ever week. It's a little slower in
blackberry pickin' time. Then folks jest will git off
and pick blackberries as the train's a-goin' along. It
makes the engineer and conductor so mad they
don't know what to do. Unk says they've got the
cowcatcher on the wrong end of the train. He says

they ain't no danger of that train ever overtaking a cow, but there is a chance that a cow might git on the train from the rear and annoy the passengers. I remember that trip 'specially 'cause we bought round-trip tickets and fooled the railroad by walkin' back!

But gittin' back to Christmas and presents,

Mammy's easy to git presents fer. She loves everything you git fer her, from a new pink handkerchief to a pair of overshoes. She says she likes useful, practical gifts, but I like to see her eyes sorta light up when she unwraps a little pretty somethin' you put in her lap come Christmas mornin'.

Sister has too much of a turn towards fancy things. I'm afraid it'll be the ruination of her some day. Onct there was one of them traveling photographers come through Grinders Switch, and Mammy let us "have our beauty struck," as the sayin' went. I never went to too much trouble a-fixin' up myself fer the picture. I never did take a good picture nohow. I said to the photographer, I said, "That picture don't do me justice!" And he said, "Lady, you don't need justice, you need mercy!"

But back to Sister. That first day we all had our pictures made, Sister dressed up fit to kill. We was a-goin' to give 'em fer Christmas. She put on a party

dress and tried to put on them new white slippers she'd ordered from Sears, but they hurt so bad she had to take 'em off. But what did she do but set 'em down by her so they'd be in the picture anyways! I was so mortified I like to of died. Vanity has been the downfall of a many of us jest like it says in the Good Book. Not that I criticize a girl fer a-wantin' to look pretty—we all want the fellers to look at us, and a little fixin' here and there has been known to catch a feller's eye.

I remember onct I went to the beauty shop myself. It was a Saturday and I was goin' to the Opry that night and was a-hankerin' to look pretty. I walked in down at the Opry and said, "I'm sorry I'm late—I jest got back from the beauty parlor." And one of them mean old boys says, "Too bad you didn't git waited on." Now that sorta took the starch out of me, but I never let on. "Pretty is as pretty does," Mammy allus said. That's nice to say but poor consolation!

Not that I was ever one to need much consolation. I've allus been a happy soul—born that-a-way Mammy allus said, so I don't deserve no credit. Some folks works at being happy and seems like some folks works at being unhappy. We uster have an old lady at the Switch that done that. Pore ole thing. She meant well, I reckon, but don't ever let her come to see you when you was sick. One or two remarks like she could make would well nigh put you in the grave. She allus said she come by to cheer you up, then she'd remark as how she was a-thinkin' as she come in that door it would be powerful narrow to git a coffin through—or she had a second cousin looked jest like you and she died. Then she'd tell you what a fine funeral they give her. I'm the first one to admit that funerals is awful necessary but they do make pore bedside conversation.

We allus liked to try to make Christmas fer them as was not able to make it fer theirselves. One of my happiest memories of Christmas will allus be fixin' up a basket fer the needy folks around Grinders

Switch. On Christmas mornin' we'd allus take the
Widder Perkins and her six younguns a fine basket
of food that we'd been canning and baking jest fer
the purpose. I allus think folks feel different about a
gift somebody made—sorta like you put somethin'

of yourself into it. Onct Sister made me a pair of mittens. They was too big and I had to sorta run a drawstring through the tops to keep 'em on, but I never let on but that they was the warmest, finest gloves in the world. I knowed how long she'd worked on 'em.

Unk was allus pretty good about givin' folks gifts, 'cept one year he run into a little difficulty. Ceph Jones come by one mornin' and ast Unk if he had a mule to spare—said the fellers down at the store wanted to give Preacher Batson something to get around on. Unk said he had a mule, but he didn't think his mule would do. "Why that ole mule of mine, Buck, is too ornery," Unk said. "Preacher Batson don't begin to have the vocabulary to go with that mule!" Unk said he picked up Preacher Batson one day in Centerville to bring him back to Grinders Switch. Unk said he was drivin' ole Buck at the time, and he couldn't come near to talkin' to that there mule like he most general done! Unk said it seemed to him that ole Buck knowed he had

him and took advantage of him so bad that they ended up in Shady Grove 'stead of Grinders Switch! It's real needless of me to point out, but that mule was jest not right fer no preacher!

Then there is my feller, Hezzie, who allus gives me presents fer Christmas! True, I have been guilty of makin' what they call "gift suggestions" here and there over the years to Hezzie, 'cause his mind jest don't seem to turn towards gifts very natural. One year I sorta timidly mentioned how nice it would be if I had somethin' purty to go on my left hand. Well, do you know what he went and done? He got me a glove—a left glove!

One year he give me a big bottle of Deer Kiss Cologney. It smelt so sweet—smelt sorta like funeral flowers. I poured a whole heap of it on me one night when Hezzie was a-comin' over to keep me company fer a spell. Me and Hezzie was settin' in the front room on the settee. After awhile I said, "Hezzie, don't you like the way this here cologney smells?" And he said, "Yep, it's all right I reckon."

And I was plumb put out at him fer not bein' no more complimentary than that. I said, "Well, is that all you've got to say?" and he said, "Well, I reckon as how I'm sorta funny about that there perfume bizness. I never have figgered out why they don't make perfume to smell like fried chicken cookin' or peach pickle—now, *there's* a *real* satisfyin' smell." I give up after that. There's no way of figgerin' fellers out. I reckon it's true that the way to a man's heart is through his stummick.

I tried that onct too. I've tried everything I could think of to git him to pop the question. They ain't none of 'em worked yet. I allus thought I was a mighty good cook. So onct I decided to fix Hezzie a Christmas dinner, and I really fixed up a fine table full of vittles. While we was a-eatin' I said to Hezzie, "I don't aim to brag but if I do say so, as I shouldn't, there's two things I can sure make and that's cocoanut puddin' and mashed potatoes." Hezzie jest nodded and said, "Which one is this I'm a-eatin' now?"

Going out in the woods to git the Christmas greens has allus been one of the excitin' times fer me. We allus git up a crowd of young folks and sorta make a party of it. Course, as far as I'm concerned, mistletoe has all the other kinds of Christmas decorations beat a mile! If I had my way, I'd have nothing but mistletoe all over the house all year round. I can't say I've ever had much luck with it, but I'm a great one fer tryin' again and again. When you go out in the woods to get the mistletoe, half the fun is a-seein' which feller is the best shot at bringin' down the big bunches at the top of the tree. I've learned a lot about mistletoe since I've got a little older—outa my teens you might say. I uster

think if you stood under a tree with mistletoe a-growin' in bunches in the top of it, that it would work like it does when it's a-hangin' over a door or from a lamp in the middle of the room. It don't. Somehow them boys ain't got kissin' on their minds on a cold December day when they go out to get mistletoe. I stood under a tree jest loaded with mistletoe all one day, and not a single feller kissed me. They didn't even notice me. All I got was a frostbitten nose and a bad cold.

It's different when you git the holly all arranged in the house and the mistletoe all a-hangin' at jest the right place fer a girl to accidently git caught under it. Not that I've had too much luck with where I hung the mistletoe—why I've even hung it on my hat as well as over the front door! One feller sure was a smart aleck—he went right past me and kissed the door!

But it's allus fun to go out and git the Christmas greens and the big cedar tree to put in the corner of the settin' room. Mammy allus has somethin' fer us to eat and drink when we git back of a evenin' from out in the woods. And we play games. I sorta lean towards kissin' games myself, but Mammy don't approve. She allus said that ladies don't let jest any feller kiss 'em—even iffen it's a game. I reckon she's right. Being a lady is powerful important to Mammy. She gits awful put out with me and Sister at times.

She didn't hafta worry too much about me at kissin' games. I remember onct we was a-tryin' to raise money fer the church and I was head of the committee that was set up fer that special occasion. While there was some that was rather reluctant to follow my suggestion, I did arrange a way to git more money than would otherwise have been got. We had a box-lunch party, and among other things we had a game where a girl would stand in the middle of a circle and the fellers would either hafta kiss her or pay a fine. I personally raised $3.47 that-a-way! One boy didn't have no money with him, and he said he'd pay me come Saturday.

We allus have a big Christmas program at the church. We start practicin' way ahead so everybody will know their part. I usually sing a song. They've gotten embarrassed to keep on askin' me, I'm sure, so they don't never say a word to me about it any more. But I know they want me to, so I allus volunteer my services. I'm not one to hide my talent under a bushel.

One year Brother got sorta smart, and I had to set him down. I didn't eat no supper the night of the Christmas program because I'd heerd tell that them fine singers don't never eat nothin' jest 'fore they perform. So I never et a bite of supper while the rest of the family jest gobbled up their turnip greens and spareribs and all sorts of my favorite delicacies. I explained why I wasn't eatin' nothin'. After I sung my song at the church, Mammy said to Brother, "How'd you think she done?" And Brother said, "She might as well of et." I could have whipped that boy, big as he was. Some folks haven't got no appreciation of art in any form.

But we have fun practicin' fer the Christmas program weeks ahead. We allus go down to the church early fer Sunday-night church and practice before the folks start a-comin' in. That way we don't hafta start a fire in the stove on a week night. I love the little church we go to at Grinders Switch. It ain't fancy like the big ones I see other places, but it's got a homelike feel to it when you walk in. It ought to—Mammy's had every one of us there ever time the doors was opened ever since we was borned.

One year they was a lady a-visitin' at Grinders Switch who offered to what they call "direct" our Christmas program. I'll never fergit that nor will anybody else in town. She was Orvy Smithson's aunt, Miss Beulie Cockwell. She came from down at Pokeville and had studied elocution onct. She was a nice lady but sorta "airish," and that ain't never took well at Grinders Switch. The simpler a body is there, the better, somehow or other. But it was thoughty of her to try to help us with the program, and it really wasn't her fault how it turned out.

The first time we all got together to practice, I got a uneasy feeling that things wasn't going too well. She wanted us all to put on and use what she called "gestures" when we said our pieces. The very first time Lillie May Fossett tried that, there was a awful ruckus. Lillie was a-tryin' to do what Miss Beulie told her to. She flang out her arm and knocked pore little Birdie Pleswell down and broke her new spectackles in a million pieces! Lillie was a big girl and strong as a ox. Mrs. Pleswell was mad as a wet hen and took Birdie outa the program 'fore you could say Jack Robinson.

Then on the night of the program, we had another bad thing happen. Little Angie Satterwhite had to say a piece, and she allus fergits. She's a timid little soul and scared of her own shadow. Miss Beulie never helped her a mite by shoutin' at her neither. I could of told Miss Beulie that, but I ain't one to poke my nose into things; I'm sorta timid myself.

Anyways, that Christmas Eve night it got time for Angie to say her piece, and she done jest exactly what I knowed she would. She got right in the middle and fergot. Miss Beulie sorta hissed out at her what come next, but it never helped a bit. Angie jest stood there, sorta frozelike. Miss Beulie hissed louder and Angie bust out a-cryin', not jest soft sobbing but howling. She was a-yellin' and screamin', "I didn't want to be in the program nohow!"

I thought I'd die of mortification! Well, that was the last time we had anybody from out of town to help with the program. The whole Satterwhite family come charging up and swooped Angie up and took her outside 'til she calmed down. Seems like we all sorta do better at Grinders Switch if we don't try to be somethin' we ain't.

I remember when I was jest a little bitty girl, Mammy uster take me with her to church and set me by her when she played the organ—not one of them big high-powered organs with them pipes up to the ceiling. Ours was a little organ that you had

to pump, but I allus liked the sound of it. Lem
Puckett uster pump the organ fer Mammy 'til he
got too old to pump. Pore ole Lem. One Sunday we
all got ready to start Sunday school and Lem
commenced to pump the organ as usual. Mammy
had her hands on the keys and her head throwed
back ready to turn loose on "Brighten the Corner
Where You Are." Well, Lem was a-pumpin' fer dear
life, and nothin' was a-comin' out of that organ but

wheezes and dust. It was awful embarrassin'. Grandpappy Bustram don't hear too well, and he'd done took off without us and was way into the second verse before somebody stopped him. All the men folks went up and examined the organ, but nobody could figger out what was wrong. Not 'til Hodge Batts's little ole youngun, Thumper, commenced a-gigglin' and pointin' at the back of the organ. There's where the trouble was all right—the mice had done built a nest in the organ and clogged up the place where pore ole Lem was a-tryin' to pump air through. It made Mammy awful mad the way everybody started a-laughin'. She don't hold with any kind of doin's like that in the church. But it was awful hard to keep a straight face when them little mice come a-squeakin' out of there and run down the aisle and out the front door!

Mammy give us a-talkin' to on the way home about "disturbin' the peace of the sabbath." None of us got a whippin' over it but Brother. She whipped him 'cause it was his turn to say the

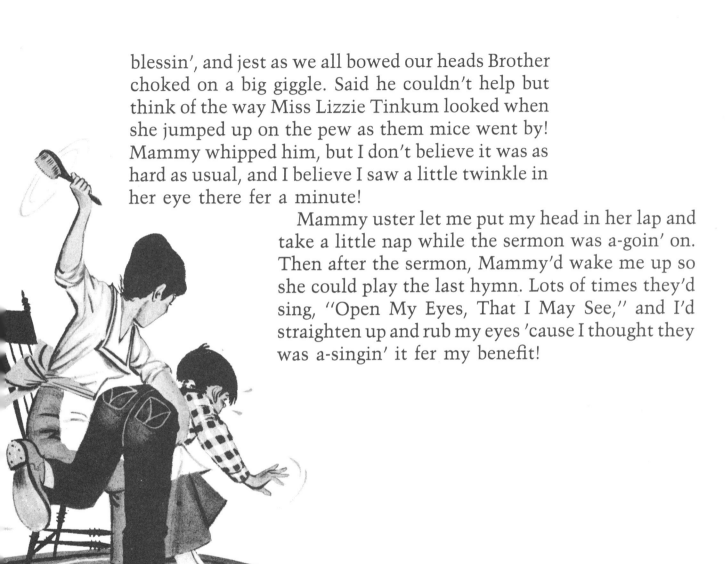

blessin', and jest as we all bowed our heads Brother choked on a big giggle. Said he couldn't help but think of the way Miss Lizzie Tinkum looked when she jumped up on the pew as them mice went by! Mammy whipped him, but I don't believe it was as hard as usual, and I believe I saw a little twinkle in her eye there fer a minute!

Mammy uster let me put my head in her lap and take a little nap while the sermon was a-goin' on. Then after the sermon, Mammy'd wake me up so she could play the last hymn. Lots of times they'd sing, "Open My Eyes, That I May See," and I'd straighten up and rub my eyes 'cause I thought they was a-singin' it fer my benefit!

Well, as I said earlier, except fer that one time when that elocution woman, Miss Cockwell, tried to "direct" us, our Christmas program is about the same every year, but it never gits ole to us. Seems like the Christmas story is allus new and there's so many ways to tell it. That was something else I like to remember from the time I was little. Mammy and Pappy allus seen to it that we knowed the story of how Jesus was born soon as we knowed "Little Red Ridin' Hood." They made us know right off the story of the little Jesus was the very most important story of all. Every Christmas, long 'fore time, we'd have that part of the Bible read to us again and again. I remember us younguns uster worry, when cold weather would come on in December, about how bad it must have been fer a little baby to be born out in a barn. We uster talk about how we'd love fer Mary and Joseph to come to our door and ask fer a place to stay—how we'd welcome them and try to make Mary comfortable and warm.

Still, as I've got older I worried a heap about that. Maybe we'd be too busy to take 'em in after all, or maybe we'd have a houseful of kinfolks and jest not have a extra bed. That's happened at Christmastime at our home. One year we had so many kinfolks at our house Christmas Eve that Brother didn't have no place to sleep, so he took some covers and slept out in the barn. So when Mammy'd read us the Christmas story we uster wonder about how the innkeeper felt when he found out who it was that was born in his stable. We allus figgered he done the best he could. He never knowed Mary and Joseph was a-comin', and the town of Bethlehem was plumb full of folks comin' in to be taxed.

One Christmas Eve when we was little, Brother and Sister and me took us a lantern and went down to the barn. We sorta wanted to see how it would be fer a little baby to be layin' in a manger down there. It was cold but the animals was warm, and I reckon the innkeeper or his wife surely gave Mary some

blankets to keep 'em warm too. We uster imagine the shepherds comin' in and the Wise Men. We never imagined the little Baby Jesus as bein' wrinkled and red and ugly like the brand new little babies we'd seen—we allus thought of him as bein' pink and pretty like the pictures of him and his mother on the Sunday-school cards.

As Christmastime got closer we'd get so excited we were hard to handle. Now, as I look back on it, I wonder how on earth Mammy and Pappy ever got all the presents and Christmas goodies in the house and hid without us knowin' about it. We 'specially looked forward to the fruit and nuts and candy that went into our Christmas stockings. That was the onliest time of the winter that we'd ever git any fresh fruit, and we loved it. Many's the time, on Christmas mornin' after we'd opened our presents so early, way 'fore day, we'd take our Christmas stockin' and feel that great big orange in the toe and that beautiful big apple and banana—and sometimes real grapes! And allus raisins and hard sugar

candy. We allus wondered how Santa Claus way up at the North Pole could fill our stockin's with exactly the same kind of candy that we'd saw in candy jars at Ceph Jones's General Store!

Christmas Eve is still the most excitin' day. We all go down to the church to decorate the Christmas tree. We allus have used cedar trees 'cause there's so many of 'em around Grinders Switch. We use colored electric lights to go on the tree now, but I remember when we used real candles on it. They was set in little tin holders that clipped onto the branches of the big cedar tree. How we ever went through those years without a serious fire I'll never know. Of course we never had no fire department then—jest a bucket brigade. Now we've got a fine new fire engine, and they're so progressive that the other day Ceph Jones's barn caught afire, and ordinarily it would've burned out by noon but that new fire engine kept it burnin' all day long!

Everybody allus brings their presents down during the day on Christmas Eve to put around the tree. It's allus been all the younguns could do to keep from peekin' at the cards and pokin' and pinchin' to see what the packages had in 'em. Then there's allus the last-minute practicin' fer the program. There's allus the worry and nervousness of "I know I'll fergit—I jest know I will!" and sometimes they do, but nobody lets on and feelings are smoothed over. One Christmas Eve during the program Lizzie Tinkum had a awful time. She was a angel and had on a white dress and wings. While the program was a-goin' on and Mary and Joseph and everybody was looking at the little Baby Jesus and singin' "Silent Night," Lizzie got to lookin' at the presents under the Christmas tree and leaned a-way over to try to read a card on a present she thought was hers. All of a sudden the crate she was a-standin' on toppled over and Lizzie with it. That was when we had lighted candles on the tree and Lizzie's wings caught afire. Everybody screamed and we had to stop the program to put Lizzie out. They wasn't really no damage done. Lem Perkins grabbed the bathrobe off of one of the Wise Men and throwed it over her and put the fire out in a minute. Lizzie enjoyed the attention and the excitement.

The one that really got the worst end of it was Luke Hodge's boy, Herk. He was the Wise Man Lem jerked the bathrobe off of. There he stood in his long-handled red underwear! The boys never let him fergit it. He was knowed as "Long Handle Herk" from then on!

Christmas Eve night we allus have a big supper with extra plates set fer kinfolks and friends that might be a-visitin'. Of course we allus hope fer snow—and they're the times we 'specially remember when we all put on boots and walk through the snow to the church, a-singin' as we go.

The church is allus lit up and that pot-bellied stove in the corner red as fire and a-goin' full blast. We stretch sheets on safety pins acrost a wire so that we have a kind of a curtain fer the program. It's a real important job to git to be a curtain puller. Brother usually gits to do that. He ain't too good at performing where he has to memorize somethin'. Now Sister's different. She shows off at the drop of a hat. She allus says a piece on the Christmas program. I've told her more'n onct I'm powerful afraid that she's thinkin' more about how she looks than what she's sayin'. Since she's got old enough to have a few fellers shinin' up to her, she's worse than ever. Thank goodness I've never been one to lose my head over fellers! I don't deny I like their company a mite, but I hope I never let my head git turned.

When the church finally gits full with everybody in their Sunday best, and the smell of the cedar and the colored lights glowing—well, it's jest almost more than a body can stand. All you kin do is jest say to yourself over and over, "O Lord, you're so good to all of us! Please help us to thank you enough—now—and oftener!" Then the singin' starts, and you really do feel full of Christmas and

joy! I love all the Christmas songs but I've got a few favorites, like everybody I reckon. Mammy loves to play the Christmas songs, and we've allus sung them around the pianner at home. I like some of the ones you don't hear too often like, "There's a Song in the Air" and "Long Years Ago O'er Bethlehem's Hills." When you git to the chorus of that one, I love to really sing out that "Glory to God in the highest," because that's how I feel! I think folks miss a lot that don't at least try to sing at church, at Christmas, or any time. I believe the Lord aims fer us to praise him in song, no matter how poor we think we sound. I never figgered the Lord to be too critical of us when we're doin' the best we can —singin' or otherwise—and Christmas songs seem easier than others.

After a carol or two are sung, we start the program that we've been workin' on fer so long. When they draw the curtain fer that to start, everybody gits real quiet and a-thinking-like. We allus have a manger with straw in it like where the little Jesus was borned. I think what makes our Nativity scene so beautiful is that most of the time we use a real live baby. Some years we choose a young mother who has jest had a baby. She dresses as Mary and has her own little boy in the manger. Sometimes her husband stands by her as Joseph. There's a look on a mother's face as she leans over her own baby that is entirely different from the make-believe. I've looked around many a time and seen tears in folks' eyes, and that's good. I'm far from a authority, but seems like to me that we need to feel things more and maybe cry a little, 'specially at Christmas.

Then somebody reads the Christmas story from the second chapter of Luke. And it's new—like we hadn't never heerd it before, and you git the feel of that night over two thousand years ago when that star come out over that manger in Bethlehem and shone so bright and so far—and the boys dressed like shepherds and Wise Men come down the aisle—and you fergit that they're Lem Perkins's

and Orson Tugwell's and Lucifer Hucklehead's boys in put-together costumes, and maybe, fer a minute or two, they fergit too, and we're all way away from the daily chores of Grinders Switch and instead we're kneeling, like the shepherds and the Wise Men, at the throne of our King and Master.

Then, after the program is over, we have the Christmas tree. But we don't really fergit how we felt during the program. Our happiness in exchanging gifts—simple gifts they are too, most of 'em—is still kinda touched with a memory of the feeling we had before, and it's good, better than jest party-laughin'. The tree is mostly fer the little folks and they do love it. Having their name called out is the most fun. We allus check at the door to be sure that we have a gift fer every child that comes in. We couldn't bear to have a little feller disappointed at Christmas!

All the little folks sets on the edge of their seats, and the minute that Santa Claus calls out each name they run up to the tree to git their present.

There's one little feller that ain't with us any more, but every Christmas I allus think of him when the presents are give out. Little Sammy Weatherby was Jim Weatherby's youngest boy, and Sammy wasn't

like the other little healthy Grinders Switch younguns. He had to use a pair of crutches to move around on. He was a plucky little ole feller though, and everybody loved him. He allus had the brightest lil face and a cheery somethin' to say to you when you'd see him at church or down at the General Store. He loved a joke or funny things and could take friendly joshin' right along with anybody. He had a special chair he allus set in down at the General Store, and he was a pleasure to say "howdee" to as you went in to do your tradin'. At Christmas we all tried to sorta make over Sammy kinda special, so there was allus plenty of presents on the tree at the church on Christmas Eve fer him. It was a real familiar sight to all of us and a big part of makin' Christmas mean more to see Sammy work his way down to Santa Claus to git his present when his name was called. He never wanted nobody to do nothin' fer him if he could manage to do it hisself. He made that clear. Onct or twict at Christmas, some visitor in Grinders Switch uster

try to go down fer his present fer him, but somebody allus stopped 'em right quick and easy. We couldn't risk havin' that fine pride of Sammy's took away from him. So he allus caused a lot of us to really think when we'd set there and watch him hobbling up the church aisle by hisself. Seems like we never had the same feelin' watchin' him being so sorta independent at other times. Seems like Christmas made it different. There was allus a sorta quiet come over all of us, and a sorta tight feelin' in our throats. I reckon it made all of us ashamed to think of how little we done with so much more than Sammy had to do it with.

He never wanted to cast a damper on things. Ever time, soon as he got his present, he'd swing them crutches round and head back to his seat with a smile as big as life on that freckled face of hisn—and you'd see the parents of the other lil younguns sorta cast their eyes at their own healthy offspring, sorta like they was thinkin' real sober thoughts. Christmas jest brings a closeness any-

way—families, friends, everybody. Leastways it ought to.

Then, after the last present is given out, we have a short spell of everybody jest laughin' and talkin' all at onct, and it's like a big family there fer awhile—and Ceph Jones fergits, maybe, that him and Lem Perkins quarreled over that election for constabule, and Mrs. Jake Satterfield and Mrs. Poke Sartin smile at one another like they like one another a mite—and that means a heap, even if it's jest fer that little while. Then we sing the last hymn and the preacher allus says the benediction, and that allus seems a little different from the closing prayer of other services—and then we open the doors and go out into the cold, crisp night and home.

And another Christmas passes, but the memory of it stays on and sorta hovers like the scent of the cedar—and even if it can't be Christmas all the year, some imprints are left. Some are lasting; some are not.

In later years I know of course that Christmas ain't as simple lots of places as it is at Grinders Switch. It ain't even as simple there, really, as it uster be. But ain't it wonderful that the story stays the same and we are privileged to go back to it again and again—at Christmas or any day—all through the years?

Have a happy Christmas at your house!